The ABCs of
Authentic Me

A Collection of Simple Truths to Change Your Life

JESSICA LY

authorHOUSE®

AuthorHouse™
1663 Liberty Drive
Bloomington, IN 47403
www.authorhouse.com
Phone: 1 (800) 839-8640

Published by AuthorHouse   10/28/2015

ISBN: 978-1-5049-0690-6 (sc)
ISBN: 978-1-5049-0689-0 (hc)
ISBN: 978-1-5049-0688-3 (e)

Library of Congress Control Number: 2015905770

Print information available on the last page.

This book is printed on acid-free paper.

Contents

O

P

Q

R

S

T

U

V

W

X

Y

Z

To my brother, Will
Mom always said it was because of my strong desire to have
someone call me "Big Little Sister" that you came along.
Thank you for teaching me—long before I even understood
what it meant—how to harness the power of miracles.

Preface

My intention was to create a short and practical book, one that inspires a new framework of being, especially in areas not currently congruent with what you want in life. My hope is that this book will be a CliffsNotes of sorts to help remind you of what can be gained from practicing the ABCs of Authentic Me in a manner that causes your own internal wisdom (and not anyone else's) to be awakened. You may already be familiar with many of the qualities, elements, and suggested practices I have spelled out here, but my goal is to share them in a manner never done before by making the content simple, easy to reference, comprehensive, relatable to modern-day experiences, and summed up in poetry to elicit both left- and right-brain contemplation and learning (or, rather, an unlearning)—naturally aligning the mind, body, and soul.

My fervent desire is that the straightforwardness of this material not diminish the depth of its virtue, especially as we discover that these qualities have always been within us. We just need to keep *choosing* the practices laid out here, as life is one continuum of choices. And as we strengthen this connection through practice and reflection, our only job is to express ourselves in more authentic ways. This deliberate and frequent expression will liberate your spirit and weave together your passion and inspiration to bring forth your inner light in whatever way matters to you.

Change does not always come easily, and sustainable change is often gradual; we rarely can pinpoint the exact moment something changes in us. But life consistently and faultlessly seeks to expand itself. Just as a seed grows out of the soil from one inch to the next, from unseen roots beneath the soil, deep-seated changes emerge in us over time. As long as we know that something is always happening inside, our lives will undoubtedly become more fruitful. It is a process not an event.

Don't measure your progress by using just your physical senses. There is a greater principle at play—one that can be felt only with unwavering faith. No one can convince you of the unfolding of such eternal joy and inner peace. It is truly something you must continue to practice and experience for yourself. Remember, just because you can't see change right away does not mean it is not happening. Please do not give up!

Much like Mother Nature herself, we will all evolve even without a conscious awareness of it—as long as we consistently practice. This is no different from practicing to gain mastery, such as in learning to play the piano. However, the sky is the limit here, and doors will open in infinite ways beyond the obvious skills inherent in embodying these ABCs.

I genuinely believe that our lives are a direct reflection of our daily thoughts and of our perceptions of ourselves, of others, of experiences, and of life in general. Thus, these ABCs of life have been directly responsible for the happiness and joy that I continue to feel in the very fabric of myself. Sure, I have my moments; there are times when I do not feel like practicing the very behaviors that I suggest here. Still, I continue to practice them anyway as I remind myself growth is a process and not an event.

As I have done all I know to embody the ABCs of me, my journey has been rewarding, and it has better equipped me to live while knowing that there *are* endless possibilities. Little by little, I am taking notice of where my life is working, and more and more I see my unique beauty in it—as will you.

I was inspired to write *The ABCs of Authentic Me* as an outgrowth of the emotional pain I have endured in my own life. I write it for you, wherever you may be in your life. I don't claim to have the answers—or any answers, for that matter—but I do know I can now experience life 180 degrees differently from the once emotionally troubled and suicidal girl I identified with for so many years. I now can experience a continuance of inner peace, sprinkled with far fewer moments of stress. If my book can expand your awareness or challenge your current perceptions or connect you to each breath in an intimate way, I know it was worth writing. I sincerely thank you for *choosing you.*

As I became deeply acquainted with these ABCs of me, I grew in the one force that expands all of life: love. There is nothing more healing than a loving heart. Love is the essence of who we are, and there is no more powerful energy than love to effect change and create greatness. With love as your guide, your inspiration, your key, your foundation, your vision, your drive, your motivation, your truth, and your life force, all is possible. Allow yourself not only to know this, but more importantly to live it in the depths of who you are and all that you want to create, as you page through and start, or further absorb *The ABCs of Authentic Me.*

May love light your way always.

Acknowledgments

As this is my first book, I feel utterly grateful to my readers for all your support; may my deepest expression of appreciation be marked not only through my words, but also through the greater consciousness of love that continues to expand my heart.

To my brother, Will Ly, for supporting me on my journey and for the countless hours of edits and ideas you supplied me. Thank you for taking the initial rein as my triple threat: my editor, my marketer, my cheerleader. You are the best brother a girl could ask for.

To my dearest friend, Brian Boyd, thank you for always being there. You help me put into creation the ideas of my heart. Your heart shines brighter than any words in the manner you give of yourself. You are a part of my soul family.

To my lovely niece Jackie Ly, thank you for combing through my first draft with such an open heart and mind. Your invaluable suggestions speak to your quiet wisdom. I appreciate your heartfelt listening; it means the world to me.

To my beautiful sister-in-law-to-be, Jerica Vogel, thank you for all your thoughtful input and thorough insights. Your brilliance can light up any room.

To my soul sister Loreli Quintero, thank you for your kindness and thoughtfulness. I appreciate our deep conversations and brainstorming sessions.

And to my good friend David Swenson, thank you for helping me find the courage to start writing. You fueled my confidence when I needed it most. You still do, by just being you.

To all: thank you for illuminating my steps with your light.

Act

As the saying goes, the journey of a thousand miles begins with one step. We may have a general map or even a detailed map, but no map can capture every terrain, bump, and path ahead of us. A map outlines only the options to get us there; we still need to be the ones to choose how we arrive at our destination.

For many of us, taking big steps can be frightful and debilitating, riddled with various usages of the word *how*: I don't know how. How can I learn it all? How will I have the money? How do I know what the other person will feel or do? How do I start? How? How? How? And we end up taking no steps whatsoever.

Sound familiar? If so, stop the incessant thoughts, and congratulate yourself. Yes, I said congratulate yourself. Why? Because you took the time to acknowledge your feelings, and that simple act alone sheds light on the most important thing—*you*, and the desires of your heart. What could be more important?

We never know how anything will turn out. Life is not designed that way. For some, this unknown is an exciting adventure, while for others it can trigger their greatest fear. You choose. But know there is one certainty that always exists: you can act with certainty—meaning you can lay the choices in front of you like a map and simply choose to act on something by taking one small step at a time.

Even those of us who think we know what steps are appropriate can't be certain the results will prove favorable—especially if we measure them as successes or failures. Having more so-called failures extinguishes the flames of desire, leading us to want to give up. We must instead look at the whole picture: the essence of who we have become along the way, the experiences that expanded our knowledge, and the wisdom that fuels us to continue when we don't always see a way. This walk of faith is our guide, and it supplies the courage to keep taking action, knowing we have no choice but to reach our destination.

Choose to Act

If and when you feel in doubt,
Step into the fear and come out.
That even with the smallest steps you take
A breakthrough you will make.
And with each action comes greater courage to be had,
Knowing clarity and opportunities start to add
To a life of infinite manifestation,
Just awaiting your choice and consideration.

Ask

Ask for what you want. Ask others for help. Ask for a miracle. Ask yourself what you can do today to change whatever it is you want to change. Ask the universe a question, and just listen … See what comes back. For some, this is equivalent to saying a prayer.

Asking is an incredibly powerful tool. Often we are worried about what people might say, think, or do in response to our asking, and we become crippled by this imagined reality. Or we tell ourselves all the reasons we can't do something before we ask; this cuts off our own legs before we even start. If we know this doesn't serve us, why do we continue *not* to ask for what we truly want, especially for things we deem too farfetched to have?

I think the answer is simple: because we really don't want what we say we want. If we did, we would ask again and again and again until the answers present themselves as a new awareness to be had and new steps to be taken—until, at long last, we've gotten what we wanted.

Ever notice how children are not afraid to ask for what they want? There are no barriers to how big or small their wishes are. And in the case of getting an answer to a question that does not satisfy them, they "why" you to death!

What is this childhood quality that adults seem to have forgotten? Children know what they want, and they are not afraid to ask for it, because they really, really, really want it. They somehow know that just because something didn't show up today, tomorrow will always present new answers in the way of opportunities.

So don't be afraid to ask. Better a voice without expectations than expectations without a voice. As Wayne Gretzky said, "We miss 100 percent of the shots we don't take."

Choose to Ask

To know yourself is to ask for what you want,
As lived by the most enlightened savant.
For he understands it is not what we can see
But in our asking as a trainee
That the goods come in due time,
And so our hearts receive with sublime.

Awareness

We all have moments when things don't go their way. However, when we find ourselves in a rut, playing victim, stressed out, and blaming others, our situations, and ourselves we are not consciously aware of the choices that dictate those outcomes. The power of awareness is beneficial in all situations, but here are some real-world examples, from what may be considered big to small.

1.) When someone cuts you off on the freeway and you are ready to reciprocate in kind—with disregard and in retaliation. Take notice and ask yourself, *What is going on inside me?*
2.) When your spouse or significant other tells you that you are wrong, and you feel defensive. What is the root cause of you putting your guard up?
3.) When you are consistently worried about your bills and finances. What is the basis for this overwhelming cycle?
4.) When your parents make you feel bad because you didn't become the professional they wanted you to be. What is triggering that feeling of resentment? Of unworthiness?

Now we are going to dig deeper. In these moments, ask yourself the following questions, and write down your answers, if that helps you.

• Am I fully living in this moment?
• Is anything really harming me in this moment?

- What conditioned thoughts and beliefs am I running through my mind?
- Have I expressed everything I need to express?
- How is my body reacting?
- Does it feel good or bad?
- How is my posture?
- How is my breathing?
- Is my energy high, low, or somewhere in the middle?

Once you are calm and connected to this awareness, make a different choice—one that empowers you. That is the beauty of life. We get to choose, and our expanded awareness helps us choose more powerfully. It is okay to take baby steps as long as you are taking them with increasing strides as you build this muscle of awareness.

Choose Greater Awareness

What is awareness in you and me?
And how do we practice it to set ourselves free
From the pain that is keeping us emotionally stuck
And blaming sheer and unfortunate dumb luck?
First we must remember to take every moment back to now
And notice the thoughts or sensations we can choose to disallow.
From this space of conscious choice we will see;
The mind will support all that we invite it to be.

Be

A friend once shared with me something that a wise and older coworker of hers said repeatedly during stressful times: "Just be." As much as we were both in awe of such wisdom, we were equally perplexed by how to "just be." What does one need to do to feel the sensation of just being? Years later, after doing the inner work, I embraced its undeniable power. Like the Nike slogan "Just do it," which connotes physical action, this state of "just being" implies action in how we choose to feel—or not feel. It is a labor in our state of beingness. It is a choice made in the present moment to embody peace and acceptance from inside out. There is nothing that needs to be done per se.

Additionally, the inherent power in *be* preceding another word does not need to be taught. For example, when we say "be good" to a small child, there already exists an internal guide to what it means to behave well. Or when someone suggests that we be kind or be present, we instinctively know what that feels like. We all innately know, even if for a split second, what it means to be here. At any moment, feel how owning the state of being can influence any degree of disharmony. *Be* _____. Be it. And be often.

Choose to Be

I get now what it means to me
When someone suggest to "just be."
It does not mean to not feel or do,
But in the "now" I must go to.
For calm and clarity I shall find,

And life is whatever I choose to design.
As I start to "be" here often,
I let go, and all instantly softens.

Breath

What is breathing? Here's the scientific definition: the cycle of exchanging air into metabolic waste, more commonly thought of as inhaling and exhaling air. Breathing, especially when done in a slow and proper manner, can directly influence our relaxation and spiritual expansion (functions of the parasympathetic nervous system), preventing us from being ruled by our unconscious or conscious stressors and triggering a fight-or-flight response (functions of the sympathetic nervous system).

But what is air to the soul? Let's dig in. Simply speaking, air is creation. It creates each moment that we get to be alive. What a gift!

To the soul, air can be experienced as life force—or *chi*, as the Chinese call it, and *prana*, to the Indians. These cultures believe that if we can control the state of our breath, we can gain mastery over the activities of our mind. This mastery over the state of our mind is the essential element for health, well-being, vitality, and conscious actions toward the fulfillment of our desires. Though this mastery, we can experience our very essence.

Through slow and mindful breathing, endless moments of joy, sadness, excitement, anger, creativity, courage, love, etc., can be fully experienced. And the true beauty of these experiences can be interpreted through a breathtaking moment (pun intended).

In this moment and in all moments, let us breathe…mindfully and slowly.

Jessica Ly

Choose Conscious Breath

What comes and goes often, like the still of the night
Yet is known to exist as much as pervasive light—
The very life force that permeates all that comes to being.
Without its vital touch, life will cease, we are agreeing.
A mark of life's miraculous nature we must take in,
Moment by moment into our body temple until the next cycle
begins.

Clarity

There was once a man that asked the Buddha which road he should take and the Buddha asked, "Where do you want to go?" The man replied, "I don't know." To which the Buddha said, "Then it doesn't really matter."

It seems so many options are presented to us nowadays. And we are bombarded with so many stimuli. We can easily become distracted and lose focus when too many choices become overwhelming and cause anxiety.

As an example, what comes to mind for me in this modern age is on-line dating. Even for those of us who want a meaningful relationship, the internet has made available what appears to be a cornucopia of potential mates, giving some the illusion that the grass is always greener on the other side. This occurs by skipping on to the next profile before really getting to know the first. Or perhaps, juggling so many at once that it is hard to devote sufficient time to anyone. This way of dating can quickly become exhausting and also yields futile results, because the focus is not there to begin with and the commitment is never made.

The opposite of such ambivalence is this—you get what you want when you know what you want. The desire becomes clear. This is the first step.

An example of this was creating this book: as the ideas started emerging, it was imperative that I became clear on my intention. It took dedicated time, but eventually I defined my goal. I wanted to write a short and comprehensive book to introduce (or remind) readers to what it takes to create an authentic and powerful life. When I gained this clarity, I knew exactly where to begin laying out the structure and distilling the most relevant and helpful concepts—as the most authentic expression of me.

It is truly important to get clear on what you want. Because knowing what you want is really an extension of knowing yourself. When you are anchored to who you are, you become stronger at weathering the storms. You become better equipped at directing your sails. You no longer pay attention to the howls of misguided advice, even if they are well-intentioned. You no longer aimlessly sail along without a clear destination in sight. You have a guidance system to direct or redirect your course. Your North Star now guides *you*.

Start here. Sit down and make a simple list. Write down what you want or don't want; this will help you get clear. They can either be tangible things or intangible qualities. It can apply to anything you want: relationships, career, family, money, etc. You decide. Once you're done … see what is made known to you. Perhaps now you'll better know what to ask for? Or what changes to make? Or what steps to take? Or what relationships are good for you? Or that you simply need to sit with it?

So regardless if you are deciding on a travel destination, the school that you want to attend, the job that you long for, the transition that has been nagging at you, the place you want to call home, the nudge to exit a relationship, or enter one, getting clear will ultimately provide a blueprint with where to start.

Choose Clarity

To that which I am not sure,
Where to find and procure—
Like the leaves that scatter during a storm.
So little I am aware and informed.
At last, my desire to get clear,
To ask myself what do I hold oh so dear?
And so the fog in me starts to lift,
I soon see clarity as a most precious gift.

Communication

"We don't see things as they are, we see things as we are."
Anais Nin

When we speak of communication, what first comes to mind is verbal communication. By this I mean we use words to convey what our thoughts are. We speak what we are thinking and feeling. Often, it can be limited by actual words and our own reality, but it still remains effective in connecting us with others.

Then there is body language or unspoken communication. This communication is more fundamental and speaks from honesty because it is unconscious. This is often expressed by the way we carry ourselves in our posture, facial expressions, breathing patterns, and the sensations of tension or relaxation in our bodies.

Lastly, there is soul communication. This form of communication comes more subtly in the ways of intuition, insights, A-HA moments, and "it just feels right" or "I don't know how I know, I just know" types of feeling.

However, if you are someone like me, you may still wonder, "but what lies at the root of it?" My answer: patterns—brainwave patterns. Such patterns affect all types and degrees of communication, conscious or unconscious.

Let's begin by taking a walk down brainwave lane, or what I concede as the tip of the iceberg in introducing neuronal communication. First, let's define neurons as nerve cells that can transmit information through the body, via both chemical and electrical means, and are measured in Hertz (cycles per second). These brainwaves can range from slow to fast: Unconscious (Delta, Theta) and Conscious (Alpha, Beta, and Gamma).

Delta is a state of deep sleep. Theta involves deep relaxation and is a trancelike, meditative state. Alpha is a state of bodily awareness and imagination. In Beta, we are in our waking state of consciousness, utilizing our logical, thinking mind. Finally, in Gamma, the fastest of brainwaves, it can feel like being in a state of expanded, higher consciousness, and extreme focus.

How these different states of brainwaves work is by synchronizing neuronal impulses to deliver information at different frequencies. Over time, these strong brainwave patterns can harden and those not used are lost. That is why habits are so hard to break. Brainwave patterns, like anything else, require consistent disruption to loosen their grip and discipline to establish new ones.

What does this ultimately mean for you? In simplified terms, what is important to understand is that brainwave patterns are affected by what we do, think, and feel. So an overactive pattern in certain brain areas can trigger an imbalance and cause problems to our health. The good news is that anything that can change our perception will also change our brainwaves. Thus being happy, joyful, appreciative, kind, and generous can shift our perception, and in effect, our patterns, bringing any unconscious negative beliefs to the conscious awareness, and aligning the two in resonance. This will help us assign new meaning and reinterpret the way we see things. It is simple—as we change, so does our world.

Many different tools and techniques, some shared here, are available to help create a healthy network of communication, such as meditation, mindfulness, neuroplasticity training, creativity, exercise, sleep, etc.

Choose Healthy Communication

Random information being sent,
Creating thoughts that cause us to vent—
With similar perception we endure,
Bad habits we indeed ensure.
To break this bond is our answer,
Preventing a communication cancer—
By triggering the formation of balanced waves,
Healthy communication strongly paves ...

Compassion

"If you want others to be happy, practice compassion.
If you want to be happy, practice compassion."
Dalai Lama

At lunch one day, a friend and I discussed the dynamics at her job. She was often confused, and even upset at times, as she explained how her group lacked understanding and commitment in working with her. She felt she had to bear the weight by working extra hours and redoing what she thought they did incorrectly. I knew that she was looking for empathy from me, and she got it. However, it wasn't in the manner she had expected as she listened for the usual "I feel you, and I'm sorry to hear that, but I'm sure you will figure it out."

Instead, knowing she viewed herself as shy and introverted, I painted a scenario that I knew would elicit her fears and inadequacies. I asked, "What if your colleagues were to invite you to a party where people, including your colleagues, questioned your level of sociability and commented that they thought you were uptight and not enough fun. And what if that happened over and over again, despite your many attempts to be otherwise? Would you start to resent them or withdraw from them?"

I continued, "But what if one glorious day you were met by a compassionate soul, someone who felt your fears and matched your level of sensitivity by warming up to you with his or her welcoming and patient nature? Would you not start to feel accepted and more comfortable? Would you not suddenly start to let your inhibitions and walls come down in that trusting space?

"Now imagine the people in your group feeling similar fears and inadequacies looming inside of them. Would you be more willing and better equipped to extend compassion to them? If you did, would this make your work world a better place?"

When you want a happier world, consider asking where you can extend compassion, first to yourself and then to others. Try increasing this compassion exponentially. How would your frequent deeds of compassion change your world? How can they even affect the world at large? It always begins with us. As is the microcosm, so is the macrocosm.

Choose Compassion

Compassion, compassion, my dear old friend
Is a quality that can only be heaven sent.
What a person of courage you are
When you dispel all judgment both near and far.
You wash over me so lovingly,
In my heart I can now clearly see.

Courage

Remember the cowardly lion that wanted courage in the classic book, *The Wizard of Oz?* The Lion felt he lacked courage and was in search of it. In the end, his true courage was demonstrated when he called upon it, in spite of fear, making him realize it was always a part of him.

Many times we go through life in a similar manner, believing we need this or that to move forward. Yet, the truth is, real courage can only come from within. It is this inner strength that we must awaken in order to overcome our fears and achieve success.

I have felt this sense of fear many times in my own journey. And when I do, I simply locate my courage by silencing the rational mind, igniting the trust within, and fearfully diving right in. *Why not?* All the while thinking, *If not me, then who?*

One of my most vivid examples of this was when I took a standup comedy class that included a live performance after five weeks of class. I took it upon myself as a challenge, recognizing that public speaking is highly feared by many. Public speaking can stir up many of our inadequacies. Our fear of being by stared at, laughed at, boring others, saying something stupid, or even worse, saying nothing at all. And, I doubled my stakes by adding the element of having to be funny in the process!

I was determined and I didn't allow any excuses as a way out. Truthfully, I was scared out of my wits! I was terrified from the moment I was asked to go on stage to share my likes and dislikes, with my beaming funny-mates rooting for me. Talk about stage fright! What if no one thought I was funny and I was booed off stage (during a class even)?!

In those moments of intense fear, a saber-toothed tiger might as well have been coming right for me. Oh, can I add I also felt paralyzed at the thought of having to listen to my own voice, over and over, in an effort to improve? That was painful. And the process of writing my own material was grueling in and of itself. I had to live, breathe, and sweat funny just to birth enough jokes for what became my eleven-minute piece. Looking back, and even in those moments, I wouldn't trade any of it! I grew leaps and bounds through that experience alone.

As life would have it, we can't authentically grow into who we can become, until we first have the courage to face our fears.

Choose Courage

What holds me back?
Like a heavy sack?
It is often fear that tells me I can't,
When all I want to do is further advance.
Cease the dialogue from inside,
And create the small wins along the ride.
Connect to courage to push a little bit more,
Until you embrace all life has in store.

Creativity

I have asked many people if they think they are creative. And, if their profession wasn't tied to being an artist, writer, dancer, sculptor, designer, musician, etc., the answer would be an overwhelming no. Followed by the belief that anything stemming from the logical left hemisphere wasn't worthy of being deemed as "creative."

What I would like to debunk is the notion that possessing inherent skills or doing something that doesn't require a logical thought process, are the only ways to be creative.

According to *Dictionary.com*, *creativity* is defined "as the ability to transcend traditional ideas, rules, patterns, relationships, or the like, and to create meaningful new ideas, forms, methods, interpretations, etc."

What stands out for me in this definition is that at the heart of this word, *imagination* is the single most important element for creativity. For anything to manifest in the material world, we must first be able to imagine such a possibility in our inner world—our minds.

The truth is, everyone has an imagination, and, if everyone has it, then we are already on equal footing. Let's start here, to begin our examples. Two sets of brothers, the Wright brothers and the Musk brothers, demonstrated creativity in different ways, but both with fervor in their hearts.

In the early 1900s, two brothers believed that it was possible to invent the first flying machine that would sustain flight with a pilot aboard. Wilbur and Orville Wright were not blessed with great wealth or even a formal education to give them a leading edge. How then did they do it? What they had going for them was a great imagination for experimentation and boundless enthusiasm. As it turns out, their extensive background with the bicycle offered a critical component to their success with achieving stability and control in an airplane. In 1903, they successfully invented the first aeronautical design, which is still incorporated in all airplanes today.

Elon and Kimbal Musk are, without question, entrepreneurs extraordinaire. In their desire to provide answers to solve humanitarian problems, startling innovations have come about. They started from modest means, but unlike the Wright Brothers, did obtain a formal education. Still, it was their unrelenting drive and imagination that led to their many notable contributions.

Elon has started four well-known companies, each to address a different need: Paypal, which offers an e-commerce payment solution; Tesla Motors, which designed the first battery-operating sport cars; SolarCity, to deliver solar power; and SpaceX, to create the possibility of a multi-planetary existence by making Mars habitable. All of his incredible innovations have been fueled by his desire to sustain our planet and the human species.

His brother, Kimbal, who was also greatly involved in many of the aforementioned companies, went on to develop ideas for something that he held dear to his heart—a deep love for food and community. He started various restaurants dedicated to his passion to bring simple, real foods to dining plates, known as "The Kitchen Community." Some of the profits of the organization are used to give back to the community via a nonprofit that creates Learning Gardens in schools and teaches kids about real, healthy foods as part of the educational curriculum. His desire is to help prevent a future of obesity.

Truly, all of these men exemplify that a highly analytical mind can equally harness tremendous creativity, enough to rocket us out of this world! In both cases, "thinking outside the box" was about finding solutions. In a nutshell, creativity is about the human potential to cultivate excellence; and the gift of our imagination includes both hemispheres working together to reap the best harvest.

So the next time you find yourself at odds and feel that you lack creativity, consider possible ideas using your imagination. Start with something that is important to you, perhaps that you want to change, improve, or impart, and allow your imagination to soar. And don't worry about getting it perfect; creativity is simply about allowing your ideas to come forth, both big and small. Just start and one creativity crumb will lead to the next.

Choose Creativity

**Eight point eight—
A logical mind bears so much weight.
The feeling that our creativity is stymied.
Leaving our imagination rusty and grimy—
Understand our imagination is always of avail,
When unleashed it will not fail
But soar and go far—
To even the unchartered reaches of Mars.**

Curiosity

"I have no special talent. I am only passionately curious."
Albert Einstein

What is the basis of life? And what helps us grow and expand in awareness? For me, it's curiosity. Why? Well, let's take the example of a baby. Take a moment to picture—or rather remember—yourself being a baby. Do you recall, even without your awareness of it, that you were curiously exploring the lay of the land through touch, movement, sight, sound, and smell? Through trial and error you fell and got back up (both literally and figuratively), developing the awareness and experiences of your own existence.

Back when we were babies, our curiosity guided us and led us to ask questions of the world. Back then, we wanted to learn. We needed to learn to make sense of our experiences. Learning was implicit and repeated; it didn't require much analysis. Learning came from a place of innocent exploration and expansion of self. Much of our behavior did not stem from what we thought we should be doing, but rather from a genuine interest. Thus it was experienced as curiosity for curiosity's sake rather than with preconceived notions. We were free to be just who we were at our very essence—innocent and expansive.

Go back to this innocence (without judgment, that is), and take time in your busy life to get curious about someone, something ... anything. And witness how much you can learn and grow in this state of wonderment.

Choose Curiosity

All we need is to understand
That life already has a plan.
And what do we need to know
To learn … to express … to grow?
Is that when we are innocently curious alone,
Life we will show us how much we have grown.

Detoxify

The definition of *detoxify*, according to the *Merriam-Webster Online Dictionary*, is "to remove a poisonous or harmful substance from (something)." For me, this includes detoxifying mind, body, and soul alike. By detoxifying, we are recalibrating ourselves to feel more balanced, to be happier and lighter. Let me give you examples.

Mind. With your mind, think of all the times you have said to yourself or to someone else, "I can never do ____ (fill in the blank)." Says who?! Replace that limiting belief with something that can be just as true. For example, "I can't do this. I am not successful." Well, what is your definition of success? Can you believe that success is not without unsuccessful attempts? Can you separate "failed attempts" from "failing"? Now try this on for size: Can success be defined as simply the courage to get back up when things have not gone your way? How would your thinking change when you accept this? How would this affect your perception? How would your reactions change if you recognize that things are never simply black and white—and that our minds are excellent at filling in the blanks and adding meaning to otherwise innocuous experiences? So, if and when a thought is not working for you, why not choose to keep the toxicity at bay?

Body. Give your body a regular cleanse to remove all the impurities inside. Don't make it a hard and onerous thing. Start with just one day. Drink a lot of water, take an herbal detox tea, or eat raw foods. However you decide to go about it, it is more important to make the process easy and routine than to make it arduous or difficult to maintain.

Soul. When you are feeling resigned and you lack hope, allow the feelings of stress to come up, feel them, acknowledge them, and then let them go. Do this over and over. If you still need to, take time out for a nap, time to relax, or time to do nothing. Just *stop everything* for one moment. Let this help cleanse your soul and move you back into grace and flow.

Remember, take baby steps, and be gentle with yourself as you grow stronger in mind, body, and soul. Remind yourself, reaching your destination is a process and not an event.

Choose Health

What toxins live inside me?
Are the stresses of all sorts what I think them to be?
Do I have clogged drains that need to be cleared?
Is there a routine of detoxing to which I can adhere?
Once I remove the debris that causes me to run slow,
So fast does life start to instantly flow.

Dream

Dr. Martin Luther King Jr. expressed, in his "I Have a Dream" speech, what it means to be moved to action by the power of a dream and the courage within a heart. His tireless determination transformed a nation we are blessed to live in today.

In his speech, this one line resonated with me most: "We refuse to believe that there are insufficient funds in the great vaults of opportunity of this nation." What this means is that those who dare to dream will eventually harvest the fruits of their labor, because they dare to believe in themselves and in the miracle of their potential.

We are all guided by different inspirations. If you don't know exactly what your inspirations are, remember what you enjoyed doing as a child. What are some things you are more than willing to do for free, because they sing to your heart and make you come alive? What would you do if you knew you couldn't fail? Start there.

But even if you do know, do you dare to dream? Dreams are not attained through wishful thinking alone; it requires dedicated action. It requires passion that leads you into dedicated action. It requires that you repeat these steps over and over, because this is what it takes to live your dreams.

Don't allow anyone to tell you, you can't have your dreams. Don't let anyone define who you are and what you are capable of accomplishing. You decide! Dream. Dream. Dream. It is your own unique path to greatness.

Jessica Ly

Choose to Dream

It is a bubble of hope you see,
Like seeds of an apple tree.
Little by little they begin to grow.
From thoughts and dreams dare I sow?
What once lived in theory comes to be—
A dream come true...so faithfully.

E

Energy

There are different ways to relate to energy. I remember taking Microbiology back in college and found it to be fascinating. Not because of the microbes, no way— but that there are so many unknowns due to our inability to see it. Therefore, I recognize that an out-of-sight, out-of-reach attempt to understand an abstract concept can be daunting at times. However, this will be my basis for this chapter, as I set out to capture perhaps the three most common ways energy is explained. By understanding energy in these ways, it can help us leverage, sustain, store, transmit, and harness its undeniable powers.

Scientifically. According to Einstein's famous formula, $E=mc^2$, since everything that exists around us is matter, then everything at its essence is just dancing particles of energy. As a simple explanation, all matter received by our naked eyes, whether solid, liquid, gas or any other form, are vibrating manifestations of energy. Everything that exists around us and within us is a complex system of vibrating energy, since energy can neither be created nor destroyed, only transferred.

As we already know, energy stored in foods, water, and sunlight, are able to be converted into energy for our physiological needs. Wind and solar power can be harnessed to generate electricity and support societal needs. Internal energy is stored in our thoughts and can either support or diminish our mind power, depending on the amount exerted from thinking. Moreover, the thoughts we put out can become manifestations of this thought energy. Energy can be transmitted when we think of someone and then suddenly hear from them. We can also receive energy and get a good vibe or not so good vibe from people. Thus paying attention to this thought energy can be beneficial to increase awareness and in our decision making.

Practically. Energy is similar to the charge in a battery. In this notion, we often use terms like "You are full of energy" or "I am low on energy; I need to recharge." And in the mist of high stress, we might say, "This is zapping my energy" or "I don't have energy."

Energy as it is referred to here is the strength to sustain physical or mental activity. The obvious ways we can renew our energy are by getting a good night's sleep, having proper nutrition, resting and relaxing, and reducing stress. So it is important to pay attention to our energy level, because without it, we may not be giving ourselves the appropriate amount of positive charge.

Spiritually: Eastern cultures believe that we are closely tied to the universe. Thus, the same universal laws governing the cosmos also govern us. We are all *One*. Everything is operating in concert and is the way it is meant to be. As such, Eastern schools of thought adopt this same philosophy; a healthy personal energy field is one that promotes health and well-being as a sum of its parts.

The first school of spiritual thought belongs to Indians and their energy centers are called *chakras* (literally, wheels) in which *prana* (energy) is passed. It is first important to understand that imbalances in energy centers aren't just about opening them, but also about bringing balance to an otherwise overactive or underactive energy flow, since the individual transmission of energy affects the entire energy field (psychic, emotional, and physical) alike. There are seven main chakras centers from the base of the spine up:

- 1st Root Chakra: Instincts
  (Survival, Safety, and Vitality)
- 2nd Sacral Chakra: Emotions
  (Self-Esteem, Creativity, Sexuality, Base for Morality)
- 3rd Solar Plexus Chakra: Mind
  (Personal Power, Personality, Sense of Belonging)
- 4th Heart Chakra: Love
  (Compassion, Self-Acceptance, Forgiveness)
- 5th Throat Chakra: Communication
  (Self-Expression, Speaking One's Truth, Authenticity)
- 6th Brow Chakra: Clarity
  (Intuition, Dreams, Spirituality, Wisdom, Self-Realization)
- 7th Crow Chakra: Connection
  (Higher-Self, Expanded Awareness, Purpose)

In China, meridians are energy channels transporting *chi* (energy) throughout our bodies. It is the movement of *chi* that allows us to exist, so promoting its harmony and proper flow is essential to a state of vitality and well-being. Thus, meridians are helpful for diagnosis and treatment is commonly through acupuncture. The meridians are also associated with the five elements of earth, metal, fire, wood, and water. There are twelve main meridians and they are assigned as a yang (masculine) and yin (feminine) opposite pair. By comparison, these meridians are like a superhighway. Things flow when there are no obstructions. In this same vein, clearing congestion will allow us to move forward.

Jessica Ly

Choose Positive Energy

Flow, flow, flow,
Are dancing particles I know.
For in the cosmos I find,
The same laws I must align.
To keep me in balance it will.
Restoring my energy, I fill.
By this mystical energy I am astounded.
For its nature is truly unbounded.

Exercise

I am writing this after spending thirty minutes on an elliptical machine. Numerous studies affirm the benefits of exercise. It controls weight, helps with mood, combats poor health and disease, boosts energy, promotes better sleep, and so on. These are all wonderful benefits that our body responds to automatically, without having to think about them.

But what can slow-pace exercises like walking, yoga and tai chi do for the soul? They can help connect the mind and the body. And how do they do this? For example, when we slow our movements down in yoga, we are forced to be more present and to take in a greater awareness of what our muscles are doing. We can further notice our movements degree by degree when coupled with slowing of our breath during such exercises.

In this space, we begin to align with where the imbalance or tightness is, and we can incrementally open ourselves up with each attempt. With practice, we experience, however slight, an increasing and inextricable mind-body connection, knowing that by bolstering one, the other will be lifted.

Incorporate a balanced exercise regimen into your fitness plan. Like a tightrope walker, we move forward as we learn how to be in balance.

Jessica Ly

Choose Health

With each drop of sweat rolling down my brow,
I feel the healing my body knows to allow.
It takes me to what I know is so dear,
Stimulating the medicine cabinet between my ears.
What's good for the body is good for the soul
In a mind-body connection that is divinely whole.

Express

"Your world is a living expression of how you
are using and have used your mind."
Earl Nightingale

There are numerous ways to express ourselves, to share, and to speak our truth and our mind. But rarely do we hear an explanation of why it can be beneficial to do so. Why do you think?

As I see it, we express ourselves not necessarily to let others know how we feel and think, but rather to declare where in consciousness we live: what our beliefs are and what we hold to be true.

Let's stop and examine this for a second. Why do we say what we say? If we listen to ourselves when we communicate our beliefs and perceptions, we hear the exact message that is intended for us. And as we do, we solidify that. What we say is not meant for the other person, other than how they choose to receive our expressions and thoughts.

So, what are you thinking now? Whether it was spoken or not, is it congruent with what you want in life? If not, pay close attention to the words you speak and the manner in which they are said. Then decide who you want to be, and express that part of you instead.

Additionally, the beauty of our expression is that it is good for our health: emotionally, physically, and spiritually. When we have the courage to speak our minds or express who we are, we don't lock in the often toxic repressed emotions of fear, hurt, abandonment, disappointment, rejection, etc. We release such tension when we share and express them, helping us to also let them go and gain more confidence within ourselves.

Finally, our expression is unique to each of us. It allows us to be creative and that is a beautiful thing! By our expression, we unleash the stuff that we are made of, and this, as well, gives others' permission to do the same!

Choose Your Expression

In how we express,
Does our consciousness rest?
For the truth we hold inside
Is what we feel and cannot deny.
And in this expression we sow
Is the one we come to know.

Forgiveness

Many say you need to forgive others in order to move forward with your life. What does this mean? And how do we do that? In the past, I found myself on the receiving end of such advice. In response, I paid lip service to the one who hurt me by repeating in my mind over and over, "I forgive you." Yet I did not feel free. Later in life, I thought I made bigger strides by having a genuine heart-to-heart, face-to-face conversation. Still, I was left feeling chained to a lingering heaviness I couldn't quite explain.

Now, after having practiced all of the things I am sharing here, I realized there is truly nothing to forgive. And in that moment, I saw vividly that forgiveness is not something to do but a state of being. By this, I mean having the wisdom to see that we all are doing the best we can with all the resources and training we have had. Everyone has his or her own triggers and coping mechanisms in order to manage challenges and stresses. It is not personal.

Moreover, I now know that forgiveness is really a cry for love. Think about it. When small children cry, scream, or misbehave, we get frustrated and upset. However, we don't sit there and analyze how we can forgive all their wrongdoings. Instead, we shake it off in consciousness, understanding they are just children; we acknowledged their innocence. Repeatedly extending love in the face of these challenges is our purest expression of forgiveness. If you think of adults as children in adult bodysuits, then the same holds true when it comes to forgiveness.

I once heard a story of a man whose teenage son was killed by a local gang member. He was consumed with hatred and had no apparent recourse except revenge. One unexpected day, he discovered something more powerful; he was struck with forgiveness in his heart, realizing that only love's power could heal his uncontrollable pain. He started praying for the young attacker and then started an organization for boys in need of shelter and guidance, where the attacker made a home. What an incredible act of forgiveness turned into a benevolent service to humanity.

Ask where you can forgive today, starting once again with yourself. For example, think about how many times you have said, "My life sucks," or "I can't accomplish that," or "I am not *whatever* enough." Forgive yourself for all the things you have done to harm your own body and psyche, and it will be much easier to forgive (or rather, love) others as well.

Choose Forgiveness

So far away, forgiveness seems to remain.
Keeping the love inside, it does contain
Until a sudden knock, knock, and what do I see?
It's the wisdom of the heart that sets me free.
By sharing the love inside me,
All is forgiven instantly.

G

Gratitude

Having gratitude is one of the easiest ways to jumpstart our emotional engine. But the idea that we need to fill our emotional gas tanks like we would fill our cars' tanks can elude us. So let's take a look at what gratitude is and why it requires continuous practice.

Gratitude is being keenly aware of all our blessings (both big and small) and acknowledging them in thanksgiving. There are several reasons for needing to perpetually practice gratitude. For starters, when we do it, we physiologically stimulate the release of certain chemicals that help us feeling good both physically and emotionally. And who doesn't want that? Also, we can touch the lives of others by expressing gratitude to them. In turn, this makes the other person feel good and creates a circle of appreciation and trust.

Finally, for no reason at all, gratitude reminds us that by consciously choosing to see the beauty and magnificence in all of life, we feed our own good feelings and fuel our state of happiness.

Gratitude will always take us back to a deeper appreciation of ourselves, for we cannot give what we don't first learn to give to ourselves. Therefore, it comes as no surprise that maintaining a healthy dose of gratitude fosters more to be grateful for. Gratitude begets more gratitude.

Jessica Ly

Choose to be Grateful

As difficult and strange as it may be
To articulate the blessings that escaped me,
I now choose to make another choice
And to listen to the beauty of a different voice—
One that works flawlessly,
Reminding me that gratitude promotes harmony.

Honesty

"No legacy is so rich as honesty."
William Shakespeare

Liar, liar, pants on fire! Remember when we used to say that to someone caught lying? It's easy to see when someone is lying, right? In reality, no. Usually we discover it by noticing subtle movements or a lack of eye contact or a tone of voice or a person's avoidance of us. Stay with me here. Have you ever caught yourself saying, "I am not pretty," "I have such bad luck," or "I never get any breaks in life." Is that 100 percent true? No, of course not! It may be mostly true, sometimes true, or rarely true, but saying "never" or "always" makes it feel true. True?

Often we are not mindful of the negative or harmful words we speak in an effort to play cool, to blend in, to seek approval, or to try to stay humble. But what is this doing? It is keeping us small. Think of great people you know, both living and nonliving, that you admire and revere. What do you think these individuals would say to themselves? How would they communicate both their successes and their failures—with loving honesty rather than harmful distortion? Use them as models.

The next time you notice a statement of absoluteness at the tip of your tongue, *stop*. Then reframe the statement to make it more accurate to the situation. For example, "I am not good at what I do at work." Perhaps you didn't perform well on a task because you've been spread too thin, saying yes to every project for fear of letting your colleagues down. In this situation, maybe you could be more mindful and ask for help or have the courage to say no and to acknowledge you may have taken on too much.

Or you can perceive your situation to be permanent. Even in this case, if you are truly being honest with yourself, you might admit that you didn't really understand something and were simply afraid to ask questions. If that holds true for you, you could say to yourself, "The only way I can get better at this is to start asking questions. It really doesn't have to be scary once I get good at this." Then you will see that as you live in integrity with yourself, others will respond in kind toward you. As the old adage goes, "The truth will set you free."

Choose Honesty

Honesty, honesty, we will not find
When our unconscious desire is to stay blind.
To all the stories that keep us internal small,
Building thicker and thicker emotional walls.
If we persist, we will remain discouraged
When the only way out is harnessing authentic courage.
By starting first being honest with ourselves,
Further into truth we will delve.

Intuition

Have you ever suddenly decided to take a different way home because something inside kept telling you to? And in doing so, you avoided a horrific accident? Or have you ever felt nudged to walk into a store you had never been in before, and met the person of your dreams? Or have you ever had a gut feeling about someone you barely met? Or you knew someone well, but something deep down told you something had changed or was going on with him or her? Or have you ever walked into an open house and known instantly it was your new home?

These phenomena can't usually be explained with the rational mind; they are felt with an emotional intelligence beyond it. Insights like these cannot be explained as coming from our intellect but rather from our intuition.

Our intuition is here to help support and protect us. Its true function is guided by the wisdom of the soul, not by the temptations of the ego. Nourish this wisdom with relaxation, introspection, and attention and it will always guide you well. So, the next time you feel overwhelmed and stuck, stop and take a deep breath. Then repeat this question as often as necessary, "What does my intuition say to do?," until the answer becomes crystal clear. When you are not sure if your intuition is speaking, know it speaks from love and seeks to expand you, even if it feels uncomfortable and doesn't make sense at times.

I believe Steve Jobs' famous Stanford graduation speech best sums up the power of intuition.

"Believe that things will work out somehow…follow your intuition and curiosity…trust your heart even when it leads you off the well-worn path…You have to trust that the dots will somehow connect in your future…The only way to do great work is to love what you do. If you haven't found it yet, keep looking. Don't settle. As with all matters of the heart, you'll know when you find it…Have the courage to follow your heart and intuition. They somehow already know what you truly want to become. Everything else is secondary."

Choose Intuition

Like a magic box filled with answers,
Guiding me like a graceful dancer,
Is the wisdom of my soul,
In which I can finally release all ego control.
I discover the melody of a beautiful violin
By listening to the notes of an intelligence within.

Joy

*"With an eye made quiet by the power of harmony, and
the deep power of joy, we see into the life of things."*
William Wordsworth

Have you ever watched children play and noticed that joy seems
to surround them? Why is that? Why does it appear that children
are better equipped to engage in moments of joy? It is simple.
First, children can be present in the moment. Unlike most adults,
they are not consumed with thoughts of the past or the future.
Instead, they are where they are. They're playing. Second, they
are not filled with thoughts of what else they could be doing or
where else they could be. They are simply enjoying it for what it
is. This is peace and harmony from within, and this is joy.

Let's look at another example: giving birth. Joy here is also simple.
Labor can be an extremely violent act where much effort and pain
are involved in order for the baby to make his or her way out. Still,
most if not all mothers are so taken over by the unconditional love
for her newborn that they instantly forget the pain and simply
connect to unbridled joy. They recognize that although pain is a
part of life, suffering is optional.

Joy can also be found communing with nature. Nature brings
out the peace in us, because nature is being what it is supposed
to be. It is not vying for attention or competing to be better. An
element of nature exists as it is meant to be, be it a tree, a forest,
a water droplet, or an ocean. Joy is pure beauty, the beauty to be

fully expressed in this moment as it is. So when we find ourselves in nature, we too get to share in the fully expressed beauty.

Where can you be present to joy? Maybe it is while washing the dishes or doing laundry or being stuck in traffic or having a great conversation or helping a friend or watching a sunset. The list is endless, for joy is not about waiting for something to happen or not happen. It is about experiencing an acceptance of things, people, and situations as they are and seeing their unique beauty in it.

Choose Joy

The acceptance that can be ours,
Each and every waking hour,
By lovingly opening our hearts to see—
That joy is our true nature to be.
When we are present to our internal song,
We see beauty that existed there all along.

Kindness

I hold dear and am in complete congruency with His Holiness the Dalai Lama in his practice of the "religion of kindness." Specifically, in his book *Beyond Religion: Ethics for a Whole World*, he gives the example of ethics and inner values without religion, being like water, and within religion, being like tea. Hence, the tea leaves and any additives only help to enrich the water, but it is the water alone that is imperative to our everyday survival.

Kindness serves as water. From the moment we are born to the time we leave this planet, every mortal being requires kindness not only to flourish but to survive at all. It is this force that makes our world go around. It is this source that opens our hearts. It is this glue that keeps us together. Without it, our world would cease to exist. This is true, authentic power. And every day provides us the opportunity to express it. From the simplest of gestures, as in a smile or a thank-you note, to the grandest of gift of being our true selves, we can all find a way to lead with kindness.

Where can you practice random acts of kindness? When are you willing to lead with them? Who can you share them with? How can you share them? Try three acts of kindness every day, and see where it gets you by the end of the week. I lovingly dare you.

Choose Kindness

Like the house of cards that builds one upon another,
Kindness needs to be the foundation we have with each other,
That even in the moments we want to just cuss,
The spirit in our hearts can transform it into loving trust,
Because if all we have is compassion to give,
Then in our hearts only kindness does live.

Laughter

Have you noticed how serious life has gotten for adults and even kids nowadays, with our jam-packed schedules? We are a society so busy with being busy: adults with the demands of work, family, spouses, friends, appointments, errands—you name it; kids with school, sports, extracurricular activities, homework, friends, chores—you name it. Everyone is so busy doing things and meeting deadlines that we are in a constant state of hardly ever being relaxed, let alone having time for laughter.

What do you think all of this is costing? Now, I am not a doctor, but my guess is that we have a lot of stress because our bodies and minds are perpetually active. I have heard doctors prescribe laughter as the medicine to fight and even cure various degrees of diseases caused by stress. Laughter has been shown to boost the immune system, trigger the release of endorphins (our body's natural feel-good chemicals), protect the heart by increasing circulation, and so much more, including something we have probably all experienced: it helps relax tension. If you are unsure about this last point, pay attention to your body the next time you find yourself laughing. It is no wonder the expression "Laughter is the best medicine" came about.

Choose Laughter

What magic can take place
As funny thoughts shape my face.
I feel good; I feel wealthy.
Why? Because laughter keeps me feeling healthy.

Learning

"Learning is the beginning of wealth. Learning is the beginning of health. Learning is the beginning of spirituality. Searching and learning is where the miracle process all begins."
Jim Rohn

Give a man a fish and you feed him for a day. Teach a man to fish and you feed him for a lifetime. This is the premise of learning.

I love engaging in active learning. With the sheer amount of information that is available in this day and age, we can teach ourselves almost anything, from computer programming, to health benefits, to success principles, to how to fold origami, to just about anything under the sun.

Intellectually, I think the most positive thing about learning is that it can change our lives, by increasing our knowledge and understanding of things that are new to us or that we could use a refresher on. And this puts us in the driver's seat. It expands our awareness. It is most definitely a powerful tool available to anyone, and, especially when it is passionately applied towards achieving a goal.

Emotionally, however, for some of us, we don't learn and instead develop learned helplessness, a sense of not feeling like we have any control over being able to do something about our situation. We accept the futility of any attempts, and just don't try. Often, this is found in individuals with depression, anxiety, shyness, phobias, loneliness, etc. The research discovered by Dr. Martin Seligman, a psychologist, and author of *Learned Optimism* shows that this condition is a result whereby one internalizes the outcome and sees it as a repetitive pattern that they cannot control and overcome.

I, however, believe as difficult as it may be to conquer this condition, it is also possible. How? By changing our thoughts and redefining our situation with a positive outlook—we can effectively build our confidence instead. So, if for example, our thinking is what got us to this dark place, then it stands to reason that the opposite thinking can alter this pattern of conditioning as well.

What then are some possible solutions? In my life, having combated my own bouts of learned helplessness, I read like crazy and learned from the messages of uplifting and inspirational books. I listened to motivational audios. I meditated. I cried. I sought help. I stopped taking things so personally. I stopped taking myself so seriously. I stopped feeding my demons with my thoughts. I started paying attention to the lessons and reinterpreted their meaning. But, above all, I began to see all aspects of life, both good and bad, as learning opportunities. In them, I began to find the beauty and grace in everything.

Everything is mere perception. The truth about life is that we can choose—we are a product of our past, but certainly we don't have to fall victim to it. We can learn from life—and grow in wisdom— that is applied knowledge. After all, if we are not growing, then what else is there?

Choose to Learn

Life can be hard,
And stacked against us like cards.
So many lessons we have not yet learned
And wisdom equally not yet earned.
When, then, does learning begin?
In the moments we take a deep look within.

Listen

As a wise coworker reminded me that there is a reason we are born with two ears and one mouth. It's to allow us to listen twice as much as we talk. One of the greatest life skills anyone can have is heartfelt listening. I've learned that no matter what the situation may be (especially in negative ones), heartfelt listening almost always creates an opening of the heart and subsequently a profound connection of souls. Heartfelt listening allows us to connect to a language beyond words. It is the conduit through which love and kindness are exchanged. And when this happens, we feel "felt." And when we listen to our own hearts, we intimately connect to Self.

It doesn't get any simpler than this, but it is not always the easiest thing to do. Why? Because many of us listen with any combination of these different scenarios: We listen with more interest and focus on what we will say next. We listen to fix things. We listen but hear only what we want to hear. We listen with judgment already present in our minds. Needless to say, none of these scenarios truly frees us up to listen and "take in" the other person.

Here are some ways to help facilitate an open heart in listening: Let the person sharing complete his or her sentences, thoughts, or stories. Elicit more sharing by saying, "Tell me more," or by asking questions in acknowledgment of what he or she has said. Listen with curiosity. Listen with interest. "Listen" to the person's body language. And listen with compassion.

Choose to Consciously Listen

Although words can help describe how I feel,
Heartfelt listening captures the essence of what is real.
It is the wisdom beyond words alone.
My heart has opened and magically grown
To the thoughts I can't always explain,
But my heart will never again hear words in vain.

Meditation

As a more integrated global society, meditation has become increasingly pervasive as a holistic approach to modern medicine. It has been taught in many countries and in many different ways.

Some have come to understand meditation as a technique whereby one sits in stillness, trying to be without thoughts. However, that is not what it is. Meditation is about having a relationship with the *present*. This helps to shield the excess, and often repetitive, unconscious thoughts from streaming idly within our being. Meditation effectively helps to design a beautiful architecture grounded in inner presence and outward activity.

The true effect of meditation is a state of being where we loosen our identification to thoughts and start to "know" that, just as the heart pumps blood, the mind pump thoughts. In this manner, meditation can range anywhere from sitting and chanting a mantra to conscious breathing to mindfulness to listening to binaural beats to yoga.

Our time spent in meditation takes us within. It expands and connects us to a world that often goes unnoticed in our busy world of endless to-do's versus to-be's. When we disconnect from this external world, and turn inward, we allow ourselves to just be, with our thoughts and all.

Physiologically, we are encouraged to relax and, as we do, our parasympathetic nervous system kicks into gear, promoting healing and the restoration of various bodily functions. It also increases clarity and the rational, calm mind functions of the prefrontal cortex, also known as "The CEO" of the brain.

This state of calm helps to relieve stress, connects us to inner peace, and awakens our soul, and thereby, connects us to the riches within. When this happens, our lives can also increase in longevity by the conservation of our telomeres (the end of our DNA strands that shorten as cells divide). Some have likened our telomeres to the plastic end of shoelaces, in that by protecting the lace from uncoiling, it prevents it from wear and tear over time.

Spiritually, meditation in its purest form is coming to realization and oneness in each moment of our true selves, our divine selves. This involves having a deep awareness of the sensations and thoughts that are guided by a loving inner wisdom that seeks to find peace and harmony with *all*—drawing our pure essence to light.

In sum, meditation is a state of pure awareness not void of thoughts, but rather focused on what we choose to think. This knowledge, along with practice, allows us to relax and heal. We master the true art of meditation by being the living and walking emanation of openness and possibilities.

Choose Meditation

Within the ceaseless noise of my mind,
In meditation my true self I find
An awakening that unleashes the real me.
That dances with life unbounded and free.
Idle thoughts no longer take space,
But rather unveil more of my unique, authentic face.

Nature

"Look deep into nature, and then you will
understand everything better."
Albert Einstein

What is it about nature that leaves us with such a calming and beautiful sense—like the waves of the ocean, the stillness of trees, the wide open meadow, the bed of flowers, or anything else in which we witness the grandeur of nature? It is simple. Nature exists in its fullest expression of beauty and does not try to be anything else but what it is. It doesn't struggle in its existence.

We will experience a sense of peace merely being around this certainty of existence. Looked at another way, when do we feel our greatest sense of security? We feel this when we come to trust and know who we are in spite of any insecurities we still have inside. And when we know who we are, we exude an energy that equally attracts others to us. Why? Because when we cherish and are comfortable in our own skin, we naturally carry ourselves from a higher vibrational state as an extension of our complete worth, much like nature.

So take some time to commune with nature with this new awareness. Notice any degree of emotional change from within. Notice how this can alter the quality of your interactions with others. Notice how the way you perceive the world can start to change those around you.

Jessica Ly

Choose to Commune with Nature

Standing as far as I can see,
The beauty of nature is so vast and lovely.
It is a calm that takes over,
Takes me a dear breath closer.
As I connect to the life that is me,
The way I would the greatness of a Sequoia tree.

Nonattachment

They say patience is a virtue, but how many times can we be put to the test?

The Buddha teaches that the root of all suffering is attachment—whether it is to a person, place, or thing. Nonattachment has been one of the most difficult practices for me. However, learning and still learning the art of nonattachment has been very freeing. Why? Because I learn to let go of expectations, and this loosens the intensity of my being and puts me back in flow.

Many of us have a clear sense of what we want in life. But when life doesn't appear to send opportunities our way, or we feel we've missed them, what do we do? How do we stay focused on what we want while not being attached to the outcome?

Now I'm going to propose a different perspective that may seem to contradict the very notion of staying focused and having a clear idea of what we want. As with all things in life, we have polarity. We cannot have a left without a right, up without a down, morning without a night. Nevertheless, such things are still a matter of perspective, and we can choose to receive it as a whole picture (i.e. left and right combined).

Try this on for size. Life could be analogous to a complex puzzle instead. There are numerous pieces. Often, we have to try different ones, before we find the one that fits. And, sometimes, we may even pick up the same piece many times over, hoping it will fit this time around, like we do in relationships. The beauty is that the more we learn what does not work, the more we better set ourselves up to find what does. Perhaps, the most important takeaway is that when we treat life as a puzzle, we can play and enjoy it as a light game, rather than as stressful attempts to put the pieces together (pun intended).

Adopting this vantage point, we can still stay focused on the goal while simultaneously releasing the desire to know what and when it will come. This liberates us to live, do, be, and enjoy, taking away all the pressure of how we think life should be. And more often than not, the desires of our heart will emerge.

Choose Nonattachment

To things we are attached,
Causing a suffering equally matched.
What profound lessons we have learned.
When the wisdom of the ages is earned.
And nonattachment frees us to live
Understanding the magic of life that does not cease to give.

Nutrition

To prolong the life of a car, we must take care of it by fueling it and filling it with the proper fluids as needed, and so on. Nutrition is our fuel, and when we provide proper nutrients, the better and more efficiently our bodies will run.

So, what constitutes good nutrition in this day and age, when the array of fad diets or even diets backed by science can get confusing? What should go on our plates? Like all things in life, it depends on the needs of each person, but a balanced diet includes these fundamentally nutritional components: protein, carbohydrates, fats, vitamins, minerals, and water.

However, I would be remiss if I didn't also talk about nourishment for the mind and soul. What would that entail? For starters, it will include many of the suggested practices spelled out here, either directly or indirectly, such as: positive thinking, stress reduction, healthy social connections, sufficient sleep, caring for others, taking personal responsibility, etc.

But so often in our Western culture, when something is wrong, we don't address the emotional component of health. Instead, our doctors would order a battery of tests be done in order to diagnose the cause for our physical symptoms and prescribe medication to treat them. Generally, this helps while they are being used but not if they are stopped. Additionally, the cost of possible side effects should also be noted in such treatment. Indeed, I acknowledge the benefits of our Western approach to health; it has gotten us far—but at what cost (emotionally, physically, financially and spiritually)?

What if a clean bill of health is reported? We can find ourselves at odds with why we still don't feel good. I have experienced this for myself and it made me more weary of what is wrong with me. Literally, I had to blend practitioners together in order to have both medical expertise and engage in open, heart-to-heart dialogues. This was when I finally saw improvements in my health. The approach was simple—treating the root causes and not just the symptoms. It was done by complementing a string of medical tests with an assessment of happiness questions. These are some examples: *What are you doing that makes you happy? What are you not happy about? What are you afraid of? What makes you feel alive? What choices are you willing to make to improve your situation?*

To build upon this new way of approaching health and modern medicine, the growing field of epigenetics, which I define as "life choices that can affect whether our genes are asleep or awake—without altering the actual DNA sequence", can address this quandary of "Can our health be influenced by the daily choices we make?" and specifically "Are we a product of the foods we eat?"

Said another way, we already know and can see the expressed (awakened) genes in the way we look (in our eye color, skin tone, height, etc.), but the genes that can still be expressed are greatly influenced by the choices we make—or don't make. Just as nutrigenetics would be impacted by the foods we eat—or rather, don't eat. So the answer is yes; we are what we fill ourselves up with, since the benefits of good nutrition play an integral part in "turning us on" (pun intended).

Choose Health

Sweets, carbs, and food galore—
Will these my body take in and store?
What nutrition is required?
For me to be alert and not be tired?
What is needed for my genes to awake?
For this sacred body temple I cannot forsake.

Openness

Openness as defined by the *Macmillan Dictionary* is "an honest way of talking or behaving in which you do not try to hide anything or a tendency to accept new ideas, methods, or changes."

Take a second to identify what group of people exemplifies these qualities. If you are thinking children, I would say that most would think the same. Why? Because children have a limited degree of fear and express themselves from unfiltered states of being. They remain in touch with the expansive space where anything is possible, and they are not burdened by the disappointments of life, as many adults are.

Have you ever asked a child a question and found no filter to his or her answer? Have you ever watched children interact with other children? Have you ever asked a child to share his or her dreams? Try doing so, and notice where they live along the openness scale.

The next time you find yourself feeling constricted or closed down altogether, imagine yourself as a child. Look at life through their youthful lenses. Write down the answers you come up with, and compare them to the answers you have as an adult. You may even go as far as asking children what they would do in your situation. Consider what they have to say, even if it seems ridiculous or impossible. Let it sit in your realm of possibilities for some time, and see what insights start to bubble up for you.

Choose Openness

Time and time again, my experiences have dictated what I can do,
Yet they have all been lies that are not true.
I start to reconnect to the innocence that I once knew
And find that possibilities ensue.
Like a child emerging from the human cocoon,
To the richness of life I suddenly become attuned.

Ownership

If procrastination is our nation, victimhood occupies the greatest amount of real estate in our state of mind. So where do you choose to live—in consciousness, that is? For many of us, victimhood has been or is our choice each time we choose to blame someone or pose the question "Why me?" In doing so, we give up our power.

Whether we consciously or unconsciously choose to do this, we don't recognize that our sob stories are being dictated by our lack of willingness to take responsibility—complete, certifiable ownership for the thoughts we think, the actions we take, and the habits we practice. We have relinquished ownership of our minds to everything and everyone outside of ourselves. And often we are left feeling stuck, lost, and helpless.

Total ownership actually allows us to take back control of life. Why? Because we are the ones who choose how to steer the thoughts of the mind back in the direction that we want, much like how we do our cars. This awareness allows us to be redirected when we veer off course; sometimes big turns are required, while other times only a smidgen is needed.

Additionally, we come to see that the feelings we feel are not our boss. They are as inconsequential as a little bump in a road. Although we may attach to some more than others, they are just thoughts. And if we stop to observe them, we realize many of them are random. Seeing them in this light allows us to move on without looking back. And with practice, it becomes second nature (like us driving our cars), freeing us to take the reins and steer ourselves back on track.

Choose to Take Ownership

We are the ones in control.
We get to decide which direction or road.
It is all in our hands,
However small or grand.
By taking responsibility for our life,
We create the least resistance and strife.
We are in charge of our destiny,
So blessedly.

Patience

*"The key to everything is patience. You get the chicken
by hatching the egg, not by smashing it."*
Arnold H. Glasow

I once heard it said that infinite patience leads to immediate demonstration. Yet I've always wondered, how do I do this? How do I give up caring that a particular something (whether it is a person, opportunity, or whatever it may be) means something to me? How?

After going through much frustration, I have come to see that patience means that the desires of our hearts will fall into place at the right time. Our only job is to know this simple fact: There is no need to fret or worry, because all is being handled, even when we don't think it is. Plus, worrying is the equivalent of praying for what we don't want.

I've seen this in the utilization of my creative activities: drawing, fostering ideas, and writing poetry. These were things I loved as a child and then forgot that I had loved them, having been in the analytical world of finance for so long. Despite my lack of effort in figuring out how I would incorporate these expressions of my heart, they somehow managed to find their way back to me. It is as though I found my way back home, realizing that life would always redirect me to my heart's desires in its own divine time.

Think of situations in which you don't seem to worry about things. Have you noticed how things seem to work out for you in those areas? How things seem to turn out without you trying? I'm not suggesting that we don't have to make some effort, but there is no angst in such situations. Now remember that feeling of ease and flow inside for just a moment longer. Etch it into your psyche.

Now consider areas that have consumed your mind with worry, fear, or doubt. What have you noticed happening in those areas? Have you found yourself filled with negative thoughts? If so, replace those thoughts with the previous one, where ease and flow are etched deep within the recesses of your mind.

Choose Infinite Patience

Heigh-ho, heigh-ho,
"Efforting" no longer I will sow.
It's time to flow with ease and grace,
For life is no mere race.
But for she who lives and enjoys
Suddenly all things miraculously deploy.

Practice

Malcolm Gladwell says in his book *Outliers: The Story of Success* that it takes at least ten thousand hours of practice to attain mastery of anything—from sports to the arts to business to meditation. No one can get around this, even if it appears they have been gifted with raw talent. Often we admire individuals who are at the top of their chosen professions; we think things have come easy for them, or they were born lucky or with great gifts. True, these individuals may have a leading edge, but without diligent practice, would they have flourished? My guess would be no, not many, if any at all, without the discipline and constant practice required to excel and to succeed in anything.

Let's take a look at why practice is so valuable. For starters, when we practice, we learn to see what works and what doesn't work many times over. Eventually, with enough opportunities to tweak and to make finer and finer adjustments, we reap the fruits of our labor.

Also, these improvements made over time help reinforce our ability to stick to it, because we see results. Practice also trains our minds to make a foreign skill more natural—and, over time, truly second nature.

Lastly, daily and gradual practice is necessary to anchor down any discipline in the most effective way and I will use the example of investing to illustrate this point. With investing, we need only to deposit a small, doable amount every day, to see our account pay us greatly over time, due to the power of compound interest.

The power in compound interest is just that, it compounds, or multiplies, over time. Daily practice works in a similar manner to help us achieve sizable increases in the long haul as well.

The trick is to discover what sings to our hearts. Practicing it is much more enjoyable because we are passionate about it. I am not suggesting that we practice only things that we are passionate about, but it is a good place to start when building these disciplinary muscles.

Simply start where you are at and start today.

Choose to Practice

In whatever it is you desire,
Practice again and again, and you will go higher.
In a battle where we have set our own limits,
We can always overcome and win it.

Present

"You must live in the present, launch yourself on every wave, find your eternity in each moment."
Henry David Thoreau

How many times have you found yourself ruminating on the past or daydreaming about the future rather than living in the present? Now, I am not suggesting there isn't a time and place to do this, but some of us obsess over such events and let them rule our lives.

While reflection and planning are indeed necessary, we need to live in the present. I believe each part—past, present, and future—has value and is a part of the continuum of life. We get to experience it all, but it seems in our modern-day world, we fret so much over what has happened or worry about what will happen that we lose touch with the present moment.

The present moment is here to take us back to our own humanity, the very essence of life. And though being present is a simple concept, it can bring tremendous calm and clarity to our minds and peace and joy to our souls. Take great pleasure in appreciating the little moments in life, because these strings of little moments become the very fabric of our lives. This intimate awareness supports us in the choices we make toward growth and expansion.

Making time to be fully present to each moment is necessary to remind us that the here-and-now is truly all we've got. No one knows when this gift of life will end. And this reminder, just how short life can be is invaluable. Live in this awareness, and life will show you just how precious and magical it is.

Choose to be Present

Here is now,
What is only to be found—
The real blessings of each moment
In its unbridled unfoldment
As I align with sincere intent,
I discover the magic of being present.

Questioning

Although I have sprinkled various questions throughout this book, this section is devoted to how questioning ourselves can bring a new awareness. No one has all the answers all the time. And even when we think we know, can we be 100 percent certain no new evidence can refute it? No, we can't, even if the odds are one in a thousand.

More importantly, why would we choose to limit ourselves to being right, when the intelligence that created life has so much more that remains to be discovered if we stay open and explore what else is possible?

So, question things not with skepticism but with a curiosity about what more is possible. This is a way to stay open, all the while casting the truth of how little we know, and how identification with certain beliefs (whether ours or others') can and will control how we unconsciously live our lives. When we start to question things, we develop an innate ability to witness the feelings and thoughts going on inside us. This is followed by the wisdom not to identify with anything that doesn't feel congruent to what we want, thereby bringing a sense of lightness to our being.

For example, let's say you don't feel good enough for whatever reason and this belief creates a feeling of heaviness inside. When you start to question why you believe that and ask yourself if it's without a shadow of a doubt, 100 percent true, you will see it is not. You will see that you believe it only because you continue to find evidence to support it.

Instead, you can ask yourself these questions: "When have I felt good enough? Whose definition of good am I adopting? Why am I seeking evidence to support why I am not good enough? Is there something I am afraid to look at or deal with? What is my definition of good enough?" But here is where it gets critical; you must begin asking yourself empowering questions. And if you so boldly choose, you can even ask, "Why am I so awesome?" sending your brilliant brain to search for evidence of that too! You get to choose what line of questioning works best for you and when.

Choose to Question

Questions, questions, my dearest friend,
Remain in possibilities that never cease to end.
I am with great curiosity in my heart
As I learn to get in touch with a brand-new start.
My time spent asking to learn what I don't know
Allows me to shed another unserving belief as I grow.

Risk

In his book, *A Man's Search for Himself*, Rollo May says, "The opposite of courage in our society is not cowardice, it is conformity."

Many people make decisions out of love or fear and often fear is disguised as being practical. Yet, progress cannot happen without risk as a component.

The risk I am referring to here, however, is not about being reckless or irresponsible. It is about being open and curious like a child who lives in possibilities. It is about taking chances, despite fear, knowing that the steps taken will promote growth and push past limits. It is having trust that what you do will bring you closer to who you can become, even when you are not 100 percent sure what you are doing.

Inspired risk is about listening to your heart to guide you and connecting to courage to advance further. Paradoxically, you will find that what is unfamiliar becomes familiar and so on and so forth, propelling you closer and closer to your end goal.

Taking risks can be fun if you make it fun. Make it a game; challenge yourself more and more each day. None of the steps have to be big, but they can be if you want them to be. There is no right or wrong. The trick is to persist and not to get down on yourself when you have taken a step or two back.

Things don't necessarily happen overnight, but practice does make perfect. Sometimes the only change might be having less fear of getting back out there. Mark your progress on a calendar if it helps, and you will be surprised how far you have gotten. Before you know it, you will see your mental faculties start to shift, and you will not want to live any other way but in expansion.

I firmly believe I cannot give what I do not have, and I continue to find new ways to challenge myself and push past limits on a greater scale to anchor down this notion of risk. A few years back, a serendipitous opportunity arose for me to travel to the wondrous mountains of the Himalayas. It was for a 10-day trek up to a summit point of approximately 16,000 ft.

Admittedly, I was concerned with the severity of the trek, having gone through ACL reconstructive knee surgery and doing very little strenuous exercise in general. Still, I fought my rational mind and apprehension from others, arguing that I shouldn't go and replaced it with thoughts that empowered me. I kept thinking, "Who says I can't? I know I can!" and packed my bags.

Although I suffered excruciating pain, exhaustion, and even cried on days, I survived. In the end, I did not complete the entire hike. The Sherpa decided it would be too difficult to get me back down should something happen to my knee, but in my heart, I knew that the muscles of my mind stretched immeasurably as a result of taking such a risk.

Choose to Take the Risk

Risk more than others think is safe,
And with belief and faith,
You will push past limits like never before,
And do what is called for,
As you climb higher and higher.
Reaching the summit and your heart's desire.

Service

I believe human beings are fundamentally wired to be altruistic and have concern for the welfare of others. However, sometimes we get lost in our own struggles and lose our sense of compassion for ourselves and, thus, others. This is not who we are, but rather a product of the many challenges that can affect our sense of self.

Maia Szalavitz, a neuroscience journalist for Time.com, points out that especially during times of global natural disasters and atrocious events such as 9/11, acts of heroism and moral deeds were extended seemingly without hesitation or reservation. This was largely demonstrated by the level of calm that prevailed during such disasters.

In my own life, during this dark period, I discovered that by giving to others what I wanted for myself, these qualities, such as compassion and care, grew in me. It was as though it filled me up inside and got so large that it couldn't be contained.

In both cases, it would appear consistent that stress is not ultimately a result of the event itself. Rather, it is about our ability to do something about it, like caring and connecting in support of ourselves and others when it happens. This gesture alone creates the feel good chemicals that help to bring about calm and effectively supports our health and well-being.

Now, I am not suggesting, by any stretch of the imagination, to be a Mother Teresa, but I do share her inspirational thought that we can all do small things with great love in service to others.

Think of the times you did something for someone and how you felt as a result. Perhaps some of these sentiments ring true: good, happy, worthy, satisfied, warm, kind, and generous. Truth is, contribution to others is not only rewarding, but it allows us to flourish personally. It is one of the core components of living a fulfilled life.

Some of the happiest people in all cultures are not necessarily the people with great monetary wealth, but those that have engaged in giving back to the world in some shape, form, or capacity that is dear to their hearts. It can be big, like in The Giving Pledge, where billionaires give away half their money. Or it can be something small, but just as powerful, such as giving your kindness or your smiles.

> *"Let us always meet each other with smile, for*
> *the smile is the beginning of love."*
> *Mother Teresa*

Choose Service

Give, give,
To live, live,
For it is in giving that we receive
And experience the love we conceive.

Sleep

*"I love sleep. My life has the tendency to fall
apart when I'm awake, you know?"*
Ernest Hemingway

Research has shown the importance of sleep. Getting ample sleep has been shown to aid in cognitive functioning, help with weight maintenance, promote emotional stability, and improve overall health and longevity. The hours of sleep necessary for health have been widely debated, so it remains unclear how much is truly needed. However, the need for ample sleep is without debate, and there is simply no substitute for getting our snooze on.

So, instead of trying to stay up and finish another project, get some sleep. The project will be there, and you will most likely be more present to complete it. When you don't have enough time in your busy schedule, see if you can get twenty, ten, or even five minutes of shut-eye. Even these small amounts can do wonders to rejuvenate your energy level and state of well-being. Stop and listen to your body, and allow sleep to get you from point A to point B in the most efficient and healthy way.

Choose Sleep

As my mind drifts off to wondrous sleep,
What healing and benefits my body will reap.
Sweetness of rest will appear,
And the regeneration of cells is near.
While I lie in sleep, my energy will renew.
My tired body will awaken even with only a restful few.

Sound

All matter consists of atomic material that is in constant flux. This movement generates a frequency depending on the velocity (or speed) and creates the vibration known as sound.

Both in ancient Eastern cultures and modern Western ones, sound has been known to have profound healing properties. The approaches for going about sound healing differ, but the end goal remains the same: to heal, balance, restore, and awaken the mind, body, and soul. These are some of the immediate benefits: reduces stress, promotes muscles relaxation, calms the mind, and stimulates the production of good hormones/chemicals.

In traditional Eastern culture, primordial sounds are recognized as Sanskrit mantras and can be chanted as a single word or a collection of words. These mantras are acknowledged to have specific rhythm that can help evoke a unique vibration, placing into motion the specific healing/awakening that is desired by calming the nervous system, making new neuronal connections, and increasing the connection to universal intelligence.

A parallel healing happens when listening to and absorbing the sounds of a healing/singing bowl (a type of bell). When played, this type of bowl creates a vibration that is rich and deep in tone and is purported to produce beneficial changes within the body by balancing the energetic field and, thereby, harmonizing the cells, strengthening the immune system, and helping to change brain waves patterns. Similarly, wind chimes, tuning fork, and gongs have been used as mediums to affect such healing.

In Western society, we often experience such healing through a beautiful piece of classical music or gorgeous vocals. Music is able to shift our emotions and change our state, not just move our feet. We connect to its words. We dance to its beat. It propels us into different worlds. It rearranges the frequency of our vibration. It lifts our spirit, moves our soul.

We can also attune to various sounds in daily life, such as the humming of birds, the crashing of ocean waves, the fall of the rain, the still of the night, and the coo of a baby—all taking us back to peace and harmony.

Choose Healing Sounds

Ding, dong, wind chime
Sounds ... so simple and prime.
To heal the body and open the mind,
So miraculously and blessedly we align.

Trust

"All I have seen teaches me to trust the creator for all I have not seen."
Ralph Waldo Emerson

Are you someone who needs to plan every minute of every day? Do you try to control every aspect of your life, thinking that will make it run smoothly? Have you noticed that even then things do not always work out the way you wanted?

Now, I am not suggesting that we don't prepare for things in life, but rather that we stay open to the outcome, especially when it doesn't turn out our way.

You may be asking, "How do I do this?" and "How do I not give up in the face of disappointments or setbacks?"

Releasing control is the same as having faith. It is about trusting that we have done all we can do and that the rest will play out in the way it is meant to, often for the best. It is about trusting that when things don't go our way, it is probably for a greater good. It is trusting that the unknown will become known. It is trusting that what we want is out there and waiting for us too. What it doesn't mean is giving up or not taking action. So, any time you are feeling drained, tired, hopeless, or heavy, take it as your cue to trust and release control.

Perhaps, some of you may be thinking I don't have those kinds of issues; I have serious problems that I cannot change. Bad things have happened in my life. Perhaps, your child passed away?

Perhaps, you have been diagnosed with an illness and your health is declining? Perhaps, you have lost your legs after returning from war? Perhaps, you have lost your will to live altogether?

Yes, life can be hard, but you are not alone. Seek solace in the kindness of loved ones. Extend tenderness towards yourself. Know that there are no unanswered prayers and trust that only God can do what men can't. And God will.

Faith is the only medicine that I know of that can heal, bring forth hope, and create new beginnings. Research has shown that the power of faith alone is the one thing that can keep us alive both figuratively and literally. Have faith.

Choose Trust

Control, control,
My enemy and foe—
It is time to let go
And let life flow.
The pain I can experience,
Dissolves to a new appearance
The lightness thus I feel.
New heights become all so real.

U

Ups and Downs

Where has life taken you? Do you feel high on life or down in the dumps? Are you experiencing much sadness or great happiness? We all know life is going to present its ups and downs. That is the nature of life. However, what may change is this: how we respond to these moments, especially the painful ones. Will we react with emotional intensity? Will we continue to exacerbate the emotion by playing it incessantly in our heads? Or will we embrace the feeling, acknowledge our pain, and move forward?

We are sentient beings, so it is necessary to experience the feelings. Nothing is wrong with that. But, especially in dealing with negative experiences, when we start to repeat this pattern unconsciously and create a learned sense of helplessness or develop vehement anger, we inadvertently lock in those emotions. We do this unwittingly by closing our hearts, because instinctually we don't want to experience the pain. For example, we learn to fear touching a hot stove, due to the emotions we had when we were burned before.

We have the choice to learn from life's painful moments and grow from them. We can accept things as they are, because we see that our difficult times had to happen to propel us into our awakening. From here we have the choice to learn the lessons that are intended for us and make the necessary adjustments. Every degree of alignment will take us closer to a healing heart and inner peace.

Jessica Ly

Choose to Accept

Up, up, and away,
Down, down in dismay—
If it is true this is life,
Then there is really no need to fight.
All will work out in the end,
And acceptance becomes our closest friend.

Vision

Consider prominent leaders, pioneers, and founders, and the vision they hold. We often consider such vision an embodiment of who they are and what they stand for.

So, why is having a vision so crucial to growth and success? For starters, it connects us to something greater than ourselves by taking us outside our immediate needs to help meet the needs of society at large. It puts us in service by begging the question "How can I make this world a better place?"

A vision gives us a purpose to live for: *what is important to me?* A vision gives us strength through the power of passion to build what we what to see in this world: *why am I focused?* A vision intrinsically inspires us: *what sings to my heart?* A vision activates the qualities that are inherent to our true nature: *how can I share this passion?* A vision awakens us to life and vitality: *why am I so balanced and centered?* Lastly, a vision reminds us that we matter. This last notion is the single greatest reason for our existence.

When I speak of vision, I am not strictly referring to notable deeds in the conventional sense of the word, such as scientific innovation, rights activism, life-altering research, or spreading profound knowledge. The vision I am referring to also includes being the living and breathing embodiment of what a "good person" is—one with many of the qualities spelled out here, such as being compassionate, kind, loving, joyful, a good listener, open, honest, etc.

And, as life would have it, our daily lives offer us a multitude of opportunities to fill these shoes by being a best friend, sibling, daughter, son, mom, dad, husband, wife, or citizen, and above all our authentic self.

Choose Vision

To my heart I must be true,
From which I am passionately ruled.
The vision for my life
Cuts all obstacles like a knife
And leaves the glow in me to shine,
For the world is my canvas to paint and design.

Visualize

There has been much research on professional athletes visualizing the details of how they see a competition prior to it. Often the results they "see" in their minds have been astoundingly close to what they experience in reality. Phil Jackson, considered one of the greatest coaches in NBA history, writes in his book *Sacred Hoops*, "Visualization is an important tool for me." Why? Because he understands that while each player is at the top of his game through his physical skills and vast knowledge of the sport, it is up to each one's mental faculties to create the focus, clarity, and calm that are required to win the game. He understands that when his players can see it in their minds, they will experience it in the game.

But what does this mean for you? Let me just start here. The truth is, this same concept applies to anything and everything we endeavor to do under the sun. Our minds are powerful, and visualizing helps to build relaxation, preparation, mental clarity, and focus, not only in our minds, but also in our bodies. This integration allows us to let go and feel good, feel confident, feel connected, feel inspired, feel present, knowing this so-called "blank state" is where creation begins.

Moreover, are you aware that we harness the power of visualization on a regular basis? We don't need to dedicate time aside for such events. Unwittingly, we are doing it all the time. Here's what I mean: every time we imagine, play out, or think through (for those who consider themselves to be more analytical) a particular scenario, we are visualizing an outcome.

Put another way, and quoting Henry Ford, "Whether you think you can or you think you can't, you're right!" So, regardless of whether we imagine, think, or feel what we can or cannot do or be, we are right, and that becomes a self-fulfilling prophecy.

So, let visualization help you tell your story as you choose the images you want on the movie screen of your life.

Choose to Visualize

See what you want to see,
However far you perceive it to be.
For what starts in the mind
Is what you will indeed find.
By fueling images with an intense fire,
The pictures of life will appear as you so desire.

Vulnerability

Think of the times when you have opened your heart and let people into your life. They got to see more than just the good, but also the bad and the ugly. They got to know you from inside out, because you allowed yourself to share the most vulnerable sides of you. And I'm sure you know we all surely have them.

How did that feel? Good? Scary? Easy? Hard? And how was it received by the other people? Did they honor your vulnerability? Did it draw them closer? Or did it push them away? Did it make them suddenly judge or even close their hearts to you without being honest about the reasons for it?

We all have probably experienced both of these scenarios: being well received by some and not by others. Right? What I would like to impress upon you is that both are beneficial to you. Why? In both scenarios, speaking your most vulnerable truth allows you to accept who you are by being confident enough to share and trust that others will too.

This also means that you will get to see who loves you truly for you and not for what's in it for them. Now, you may need to change some parts that you don't like or may not desire in your life, but this will allow for others to support you in being the best version of yourself along the way.

Jessica Ly

Choose Vulnerability

Being me for me …
Authentically free.
My walls start to come down,
For it is my own true value I've finally found.
And no longer will I need to hide;
For all to see me with arms open wide.

Walk

"Everyone has his own specific vocation or mission in life; everyone must carry out a concrete assignment that demands fulfillment. Therein he cannot be replaced, nor can his life be repeated, thus, everyone's task is unique as his specific opportunity to implement it."
Viktor E. Frankl

How often do you find yourself comparing what you have to what another person has? More often than not, I would guess. And how often do you measure them against someone you feel is better off in life? Too many, perhaps. I know I have been guilty as charged.

But as soon as I had the courage to start walking my own path, the comparisons to others gradually started to fade. I started to feel more connected to my true purpose, and it really didn't matter what other people may or may not be doing better than me. Indeed, it helped that I was passionately working toward something that spoke to my heart. This passion created such an engaged focus, time would often fly by, because I was joyously just doing it.

I understand that we all have to start somewhere, and the key is to have the courage to start. It's amazing that with every little step taken, our confidence builds like a muscle. Better yet, we will look back and find that it is not nearly as scary as we initially made it out to be. Or even if it was, the good feelings that accompanied the steps taken will reign over any negative ones. Simply put, confidence grows as you do. It doesn't work the other way around.

Jessica Ly

Choose Your Unique Path

Take the first step you know
And continue to walk ... if you must, slow.
It doesn't matter either way,
So long as you stay out and play.
For in your own path you will find
A story of greatness that has always been yours to define.

Xerox

You may not know what you want. And that is okay. Until you do, think about who you would like to see yourself as and the things you will stand for that mean something to you. You can think of any ideals or innovations of a role model you resonate with.

You may have several role models; in that case, take whatever you like from each. You can blend all those qualities and make them your own. In all ways, regardless of how many role models you have, you will always bring your own uniqueness; after all, there is and will always be only one of you. So, go out and express it!

Choose a Mentor or Role Model

Who do I want to be, who do I want to be?
Let me find a role model until it is clear to me
That the person that lies inside
Is the real me that I can no longer deny.
She will come forth as her very own
And give the gifts she has so fervently sown.

Yes!

Someone once shared with me a very powerful tool. It was to say yes to life—all of it. Where in your life can you start putting yes to the test? Where in your life have you been afraid to say yes? Saying yes does not mean doing something just to do it or if you really hate it. For example, if someone offered you green-tea ice cream, and you don't like it, then don't eat it.

The yes I am referring to here comes from passion for life, or at the very least a willingness to venture outside your comfort zone. Try things anyway, despite having emotions like fear or failure or rejection. For example, if there is a woman behind the Starbucks counter that you have been afraid to talk to, take a chance, be courageous, and start talking.

We are given the chance here to write our ultimate story! Pretend to be at the end of your life, looking back. It doesn't matter if you are seventeen, twenty-two, forty-five, sixty-one, or eighty-eight—just imagine yourself there with me.

Life is not set in stone, and although the desires of our hearts and lessons presented to us to learn may reappear, it is not predestined to the degree that we have free will to choose our habits and attitude. We can always change our minds along the journey. For now, just let yourself be here and now, as you are. Ready?

How do you want your life to look? What stories would you like to experience? What would you do if you knew you couldn't fail? What makes you come alive? How can you help others? How do you want to be remembered? And, most importantly, how can you extend love? Step into this awareness as you contemplate these questions. And with this openness, allow it to happen with a *big fat yes!*

Choose Yes

The power of yes cannot be defined.
But adventure you will get when you are unconfined.
For the love of life is found
When yes is your answer all around.

Zillion

Alexander Graham Bell said, "When one door closes, another opens; but we often look so long and so regretfully upon the closed door that we do not see the one which has opened for us."

How many times have you found yourself here, looking at a closed door? Down on yourself and down on hope. Wondering is this it? Is this all there is to life?

Les Brown, the world's leading motivational speaker and author, defines the difference between eyesight and mindsight in his "It's Possible" speech. Eyesight is judging on what you see and mindsight is how you interpret what you see. This powerful distinction is a game changer. We don't need to subscribe to the conditions of our world through eyesight. Rather we can choose to write our own stories using our mindsight.

Because I don't know what I don't know, I am left with just this simple but powerful tool: to believe. So don't see with just your eyes, but see with all your heart, that you too can create the possibilities for your life.

I found that my expansion in consciousness has helped me replace the often elusive *"need to understand"* for the *"clear intention to see."* So when I stay open and ask, a new door will eventually present itself, because I *"see"* it for myself.

You must choose to "see" it for yourself!

This truly is magical. When I recognize I am stuck and ask for answers, they always come in the manner they are intended to come. Often, I do have to be patient and persistent. But, because I choose to live believing there are a zillion possibilities, I stay open.

We really don't know what life has in store for us, so believe in yourself and please don't give up! Know deep down at the cellular level that it is possible! The Universe has your back!

Try it, and watch as the proverbial door of possibilities opens for you.

Choose Endless Possibilities

I don't know what I will find,
But to new doors I will no longer stay blind.
For I cannot see what I don't know,
And life remains without flow.
It is clear I see that this is my only task.
In new possibilities I will start to ask,
And doors will begin to open.
For the Universe has my constant devotion!

Eternal Salvation

My heart opens without fear,
As the dawn of my spirit draws near.
A search for inner peace inspires my healing.
Upon reaching my miserable emotional ceiling.
With wings that were previously broken,
Serving to remind me that life is but a silver token.
Whereas I was formerly lost,
The joy of my existence did it painfully cost.
A commitment to my soul's evolution,
Marks the beginning of this sacred restitution.
In deepening meditations,
I release the mind of these insidious invasions.
In accepting the is-ness of all people and things.
Did inner peace stem forward and beautifully spring.
In perpetual thanksgiving and genuine gratitude,
Was there an unveiling of a divine and idyllic attitude.
In the removal of the barriers to love,
Did my soul return to this proverbial dove.
In non-judgment and complete stillness,
I was able to slowly dissolve all this mental illness.
The stories that I have held on to so tirelessly,
Of poor, poor me with such intensity.
Leaves the young girl that was once tightly wounded.
Now emerges as a renewed energy forever unbounded.
The personality that I thought was so kindly giving;
Was not from the overflow in which I was unconsciously living.
No longer are my thoughts of lack and not enough-ness,
Rather, ridding of the façade and perceived toughness.
My soul journeys back home.

From which I have aimlessly roamed.
Finds me seeing with only love in my heart,
As I look upon myself, others, and this world with a new authentic start.
Thus, my timeless creativity blossoms from within,
An expression of the confidence I feel inside my own skin.
The external is but a mere reflection of the thoughts held inside.
As the laws of the universe always complies.
My profound awakening is a "knowing" to me,
That I now hold for others to see.
With unwavering practice and sincere dedication,
All too, can discover true freedom, and thereby, eternal salvation

Final Words

"Love recognizes no barriers. It jumps hurdles, leaps fences,
penetrates walls to arrive at its destination full of hope."

These words of heart-centered wisdom by Maya Angelou best
sum up the gifts of embodying these ABCs. My deepest wish for
you is that through these practices you will live in the hearts of
others with this exact distinction.

About the Author

Jessica Ly is a life coach, meditative breathing teacher, and devout poet. She graduated from the University of Southern California with a B.S. in Exercise Science. She values experiential and cognitive learning found in the integration of physiological, spiritual, and mental awareness and teaches it through a set of practices she calls Meditative Breathing for Alignment.

She teaches at Common Ground Spiritual Wellness Center, the Marine Corps, the Wounded Warrior Battalion West, along with various other organizations. She also blogs for the Huffington Post and Transcendental Meditation sites.

Jessica has taken her own personal journey to meditate with Buddhist monks in the Himalayas and loves travelling to enrich her own connection to communities around the world. She believes it is not so much about gaining knowledge, but living it that leads to infinite peace and joy—and the empowerment of leadership and great change.

www.jessicaly.me
www.awakenyoursoul1.com

Dearest Incredible Ones,

Thank you again for allowing me to be a part of your journey. I appreciate the time you have spent reading this book and would love to hear from you. Please email me at ABCs.Authentic.Me@gmail.com and let me know what letter(s) spoke to you, any concepts or ideas for future discussion, or anything else you would like to share. My door is open!

In Love, In Service,
Jessica Ly

Printed in the United States
By Bookmasters